Watermelons and Muskmelons in South Dakota

by N.E. Hansen, Horticulturist, Department of Horticulture,
W.S. Thornber, Assistant, Department of Horticulture,
U.S. Department of Agriculture

with an introduction by Roger Chambers

This work contains material that was originally published in 1900.

This publication was created and published for the public benefit,
utilizing public funding and is within the Public Domain.

This edition is reprinted for educational purposes
and in accordance with all applicable Federal Laws.

Introduction Copyright 2017 by Roger Chambers

Self Reliance Books

Get more historic titles on animal and stock breeding, gardening and old fashioned skills by visiting us at:

http://selfreliancebooks.blogspot.com/

Introduction

I am pleased to present yet another title on Gardening.

The work is in the Public Domain and is re-printed here in accordance with Federal Laws.

As with all reprinted books of this age that are intended to perfectly reproduce the original edition, considerable pains and effort had to be undertaken to correct fading and sometimes outright damage to existing proofs of this title. At times, this task is quite monumental, requiring an almost total "rebuilding" of some pages from digital proofs of multiple copies. Despite this, imperfections still sometimes exist in the final proof and may detract from the visual appearance of the text.

I hope you enjoy reading this book as much as I enjoyed making it available to readers again.

Roger Chambers

WATERMELONS AND MUSKMELONS IN 1898-99.

DEPARTMENT OF HORTICULTURE.

N. E. HANSEN,
  Horticulturist.

W. S. THORNBER,
  Assistant.

In the northern part of this State the need of early varieties of melons, especially watermelons, is generally felt. In specially favorable soils and locations little difficulty is experienced, but on dry upland with ordinary field cultivation, the season of maturity of watermelons is too near the time of killing frosts.

Watermelons are more appreciated during hot weather than when cool weather sets in. Can an extra early variety of watermelon be bred to meet this want? This question was brought to mind with especial force to the horticulturist of this department during a ten-months' trip (June, 1897-March, 1898,) collecting seeds for the United States Department of Agriculture in European Russia and Central Asia. In the Volga river region good watermelons are grown north of the corn belt of southern Russia. Numerous large barges were noted on the Volga river filled with watermelons. The land is largely summer-fallowed in alternate years, and some of the best fields are used for melons as a resting crop in the summer-fallow year.

Upon reaching Transcaucasia, north of Armenia, between the Black and Caspian seas, extra large muskmelons were observed, especially in the region near Mount Ararat. But it was not until the cotton-growing sections east of the Caspian sea, in Turcomania, Bokhara, Amu Daria, Samarkand and Tashkend, all in Russian Turkestan, just north of Persia and

Afghanistan and west of China, was reached, that the climax in size of muskmelons was observed. Ordinary specimens of many varieties weighed fully thirty pounds, as purchased in the bazars, and government officials informed me that select specimens often weighed over one Russian pood (equals thirty-six pounds avoirdupois) each.

Some varieties do not ripen on the vines, but are hung up in slings in the houses close to the ceiling and ripen through the winter and spring.

Seeds of 287 varieties of muskmelons and watermelons were obtained for trial in the United States, and have been distributed by the U. S. Department of Agriculture. (See Inventory Nos. 1 and 2, U. S. Department of Agriculture, Section of Seed and Plant Introduction). The large winter muskmelons from Turkestan have done well so far only in the warm dry sections of the United States, which is probably due to the fact that they are mostly from cotton-growing regions. Their long-keeping capacity and excellent quality are bringing some of them into prominence in Colorado and elsewhere.

During the past two years, varieties of melons (including a few strains of the same variety) have been planted at this Station, as follows:

	1898	1899
American watermelons	35	100
Imported watermelons	63	59
American muskmelons	37	153
Imported muskmelons	114	90

The results are, briefly:

1. The American muskmelons are much better adapted to this locality than any of the foreign varieties tested.

2. Among the Russian watermelons one was found superior in earliness to any of the American varieties tested.

3. From the earliest watermelon pure seed was grown. By continued selection we hope to increase the earliness of this variety, and in due season to distribute surplus seed for trial elsewhere.

MELONS IN 1898.

In the spring of 1898, a suitable piece of land was rented near the Station grounds. The soil was a rich, black, somewhat sandy loam, underlaid about one foot deep with a hard boulder clay subsoil. The land was rather high and dry with a gentle west slope, and had been continuously in grain crops, chiefly wheat, for the past eighteen or twenty years. It was by no means an ideal location for melons, but fairly typical of the ordinary farm garden in this vicinity. No manure or fertilizer of any kind was applied, and only good ordinary field cultivation given, the aim being to give only such care as every farmer can give with many acres of farm crops under cultivation. The work of planting and cultivation was carefully done by Mr. Adam P. Thornber.

Ninety-eight varieties of watermelons were planted May 19th in hills 6x8 feet. Of these 35 were standard American varieties, 56 imported direct from European and Asiatic Russia by the United States Department of Agriculture, 6 from a Russian settlement in Minnesota, and 1 obtained while in Kursk, Russia, in 1894. The season was very unfavorable. Dry weather retarded germination, cool nights hindered rapid growth and killing frosts came the first week in September. It was a very severe test and any variety ripening under such conditions may be regarded as safe to plant in this locality.

The 5 best varieties in order of earliness were United States Department of Agriculture Nos. 23, 32, 16, 19, 79. United States Department No. 23 ripened perfectly and was a red-fleshed melon of excellent quality.

WATERMELONS, 1898.

AMERICAN VARIETIES.

NAME.	HILLS.		SIZE OF FRUIT DIAMETERS IN INCHES.		Maturity.	REMARKS.
	Planted.	Grew.	Length.	Breadth.		
Black Diamond	2	2	7.	6.25	Green	
Black Spanish	2	2	7.	6.5	Green	
Cole's Early	20	20	8.5	7.	Turning	
Colorado Citron	2	2	8.	8.	Green	
Cuban Queen	2	2	7.5	7.	Green	Vines 18 feet long
Dark Icing	2	2	7.	6.25	Green	
Dixie	4	4	9.5	7.5	Turning	
Duke Jones	2	2	6.5	6.25	Very green	
Florida's Favorite	2	1	4.5	4.	Green	
Fordhook Early	10	10	9.	8.	Turning	
Girardeau's Favorite	2	2	12.5	5.25	Turning	
Hoosier King	2	2	8.	8.	Green	
Hungarian Honey	2	2	6.	6.	Green	
Jones Jumbo	2	1			Green	
Kentucky Wonder	2	2	8.	6.25	Green	
Kansas Stock	2	2	9.5	4.5	Green	
Kolb's Gem	2	2	8.75	7.	Green	
Kleckley's Sweet	2	2	10.	5.5	Green	
Long White Icing	2	2	6.5	5.5	Green	
McIver's Wonderful Sugar	2	1	9.	5.5	Green	
Mountain Sweet	2	2	8.	5.5	Green	
New Triumph	2	2	7.5	7.	Green	
Phinney's Improved	2	2	11.	6.5	Green	
Rattlesnake	2	2	13.	5.5	Turning	
Red Seeded Citron	2	2	7.	6.5	Green	
Seminole	2	2	8.25	5.5	Green	
Sweetheart	2	2	6.	5.	Green	
True Ice Cream	2	2	9.	7.	Green	
Volga	30	30	7.5	7.25	Turning	
Salzer's White Rind	5	5	7.	7.	Green	
Salzer's Wonderful Sugar	5	5	11.5	6.5	Green	
Salzer's Fourth of July	5	5	6.	6.	Turning	
Salzer's Sweetheart	5	5	5.5	5.5	Green	
Salzer's Earliest	5	5	7.5	7.	Turning	
Salzer's Golden Rind	2	2	7.5	7.	Almost ripe	Promising

WATERMELONS, 1898.

FOREIGN VARIETIES

U. S. Dept. No.	NAME.	HILLS. Planted.	HILLS. Grew.	SIZE OF FRUIT DIAMETERS IN INCHES. Length.	SIZE OF FRUIT DIAMETERS IN INCHES. Breadth.	Maturity.	REMARKS.
16	....	2	2	12.	6.5	Nearly ripe	Promising
18	....	2	1	8.	7.5	Turning	
20	....	2	2	8.	8.	Green	
22	....	2	2	8.5	7.5	Turning	
23	....	2	2	7.5	7.	Ripe	Flesh red, sweet, the earliest
24	....	2	2	14.5	6.	Turning	
25	....	2	2	6.5	5.5	Green	
26	....	2	2	8.	6.5	Turning	
29	....	2	2	8.5	8.5	Turning	
32	....	2	2	7.	6.5	Nearly ripe	Promising
33	....	2	2	7.	6.5	Turning	
35	....	2	2	7.	6.5	Turning	Of some promise
40	....	2	2	6.	6.	Green	
43	....	2	2	6.5	6.5	Turning	
44	....	2	2	7.	7.	Green	
45	....	2	2	6.	4.5	Green	
46	....	2	2	8.5	5.5	Green	
47	....	2	2	7.	6.5	Too late	Two ripe out of 8; yellow flesh
48	....	2	2	7.5	6.5	All turning	Flesh red when very small
49	....	2	2	8.	7.	Green	Two types
50	....	2	1	7.	5.5	Green	
55	....	2	2	5.5	5.	Turning	
61	....	2	2	13.	6.	Green	Two types, long and round
64	....	2	2	7.	5.5	Turning	Four types
68	....	2	2	7.5	7.	Green	
69	....	2	2	7.	6.5	Turning	
70	....	2	1	10.	6.	Turning	
71	....	2	2	....	....	Turning	
72	....	2	2	7.5	7.	Turning	
73	....	2	2	8.75	8.	Green	
74	....	2	2	7.75	6.75	Turning	
75	....	2	2	5.	4.5	Green	
76	....	2	2	5.	4.5	Green	
77	....	2	2	10.5	5.5	Turning	
79	....	2	1	6.25	5.75	Turning	
80	....	2	2	6.	6.	Green	

WATERMELONS, 1898.

FOREIGN VARIETIES.

U. S. Dept. No.	NAME.	HILLS.		SIZE OF FRUIT DIAMETERS IN INCHES.		Maturity.	REMARKS.
		Planted.	Grew.	Length.	Breadth.		
82	....	2	2	6.	5.5	Green.	....
84	....	2	0	....	....	......	....
85	....	2	2	5.5	5.	Green	....
86	....	2	2	6.5	5.	Green	....
87	....	2	2	7.25	6.	Green	....
88	....	2	2	8.5	7.	Turning	....
89	....	2	1	6.5	6.	Green	....
90	....	2	2	8.	5.	Turning	....
91	....	2	1	....	....	Green	....
92	....	2	2	8.	5.	Green	....
93	....	2	2	6.	5.5	Green	....
94	....	2	2	6.	5.	Green	....
102	....	2	2	6.5	6.	Green	....
104	....	2	1	8.	7.5	Green	One fruit ripe, 2 nearly ripe
105	....	2	2	7.	7.	Nearly ripe	Fruit just formed
106	....	2	1	8.5	7.	Turning	Fruit just formed
836	....	2	3	....	....	......	....
866	....	4	10	8.5	7.	Turning	....
....	From Samara, Russia......	10	10	....	....	Green	....
....	From Bokhara, Turkestan..	2	2	....	....	......	....
....	Russian Mennonite No. 6..	3	3	6.5	6.	Turning	Type mixed, 2 ripe out of 24
....	Russian Mennonite No. 7..	2	2	8.	7.	Green	Mixed type
....	Russian Mennonite No. 8..	2	0	....	....	......	....
....	Russian Mennonite No. 9..	4	4	8.	7.	Green	....
....	Russian Mennonite No. 10.	2	0	....	....	......	....
....	Russian Mennonite No. 11.	2	2	8.	6.5	Green	Mixed type, 1 ripe out of 11
....	No. 1 Kursk, Russia, 1894 seed	2	2	8.	7.	Green	....
....	1896 seed of No. 1 Kursk...	2	2	6.5	6.	Green	....
....	1897 seed of No. 1 Kursk...	2	2	7.5	7.	Green	....

MUSKMELONS, 1898.

One hundred and fifty-one varieties of muskmelons were planted May 19, 1898, including 37 American varieties and 114 sorts imported from European Russia and Central Asia (Russian Turkestan). The season was very unfavorable and killing frosts came the first week in September.

Two hills were planted of each of the following, but no vines were obtained; the seed either failed to germinate or the plants were destroyed by insect enemies:

U. S. Dept. Nos. 15, 28, 27, 17, 30, 31, 34, 35, 36, 37, 53, 56, 81, 99, 97, 110, 114, 115, 117, 118, 119, 120, 124, 125, 132, 135, 140, 136, 141, 142, 153, 154, 155, 162, 158, 163, 165, 166, 169, Baltimore Acme, Cosmopolitan, Round Netted Gem, Russian Mennonite Nos. 3 and 4. Ten hills of Bokhara No. 8; same result.

Two hills were planted of each of the following; one or both hills grew, but no fruit formed:

U. S. Dept. Nos. 19, 21, 51, 38, 59, 96, 101, 108, 109, 116, 121, 122, 123, 130, 127, 128, 129, 138, 137, 143, 144, 145, 152, 149, 150, 157, 161, 164, 54, 134, 139, 146, 156, 160, 172, Bokhara No. 2, Chicago Market Ordinary, Improved Cantaloupe, New Cannon Ball, Superior.

Ten hills each of Bokhara Nos. 1, 3, 4, 5, 6, 7, and Turkestan mixed (Zablotsky); no fruit formed.

Twenty hills of Osage were planted, 11 grew; no fruit.

Two hills were planted of each of the following; one or both hills grew, but the fruit was just formed when caught by frost:

Banana, Banquet, Bay View, Champion Market, Delmonico, Emerald Gem, Extra Early Giant Prolific, Extra Early Hackensack, Extra Early Nutmeg, Green Fleshed Osage, Hackensack, Ironclad, Irondequoit, Long Island Beauty, Melrose, New Orleans Market, Osage Select, Shumway's Giant, Thorburn's Giant, Tip Top, Vaughan's Select True Jenny Lind, Grand Rapids. U. S. Dept. Nos. 63, 60, 78, 107, 126, 133, 168, 66, 83, 131, 159, 167. Ten hills of Bokhara No. 9 planted; four hills grew; same result.

Two hills were planted of each of the following. One or both hills germinated and fruit obtained, but none ripened satisfactorily. U. S. Dept.. Nos. 39, 42, 52, 57, 62, 65, 95, 98, 100, 103, 147, 170, 171; Russian Mennonite (Windom, Minn.,) Nos. 1, 2, 5. Early Nutmeg, Giant Chicago Market, Montreal Market Nutmeg, Newport, Princess, Perfection. Same result from 18 hills of Oval Netted Gem. In general the American varieties were much nearer maturity than the foreign sorts and showed their better adaptation to prairie conditions in an unfavorable season.

MELONS IN 1899.

The same piece of land was used as in 1898. The watermelons were planted May 24 and the muskmelons May 25 and 26, in hills 7x7 feet apart, and thinned to 3 vines in each hill. Of watermelons 100 American and 59 imported varieties were planted, and of muskmelons 153 American and 90 imported varieties were planted. Of these, 32 varieties of imported muskmelons, two varieties of imported watermelons and one of American watermelons, failed to germinate or were destroyed by insects, and 12 were duplicates from various sources, leaving a net total of 199 varieties of muskmelons and 154 of watermelons on trial. Good, ordinary field cultivation was given and no fertilizers applied, the same as the previous year. The work of planting and cultivation was carefully done by Mr. Adam P. Thornber. The season was more favorable, and killing frost did not come until September 16. The American muskmelons as a class yielded a large crop, and none of the imported varieties equalled them in earliness or productiveness. The squash beetle and root-borer worked more on the foreign than on the American varieties. If started under glass on sods, or in pots, it may be that some of these choice Turkestan winter muskmelons may be fruited in this latitude, but they are certainly not adapted to field cultivation.

The results with watermelons were better than in the

previous year, but still the fact was clearly brought out that we need earlier varieties. Any variety not fully ripe during the first week of September under field cultivation is not early enough.

U. S. Dept. of Agr. No. 23 again showed its superior earliness, the first fruit ripening August 24. It was determined to raise some pure seed of this variety. As only a few seeds were left of the original package after planting four hills in the field, they were planted singly in pots in the greenhouse May 24, transplanted into rich soil in the garden June 23, and watered when needed. This method increased the size and weight considerably (from 7x7 inches to 14x13 inches, and from 4 lbs. 4 ozs. to 14 lbs. 8 oz.,) and the earliness 9 days, the first fruit ripening August 15 (shown in plate No. 3). In both lots variations from the type appeared, all early, with thin rind and red flesh. The most marked deviation in shape is shown in Plate 1. The true very early type is shown in Plate 3. The seed obtained from the lot grown separate in 1899 will, we hope, give sufficient seed in 1900 for distribution for trial elsewhere in 1901. "Pjatigorsk" means "Five-mountain" but even when translated, the name "Favorite of the Five-Mountain Farm" will need abbreviation or modification to make it acceptable to American tongues. It is not the same as U. S. Dept. Nos. 20, 43 and 105, which bear the same name.

By careful selection for a number of years we hope to increase the earliness of U. S. Dept. No. 23, which has proved to be the earliest variety tested in our two years' trial.

In the tables the names of the seedsmen from whom the American varieties were obtained are abbreviated. The following gives the names in full:

Burpee, W. Atlee Burpee & Co., Philadelphia, Penn.; Gregory, J. J. H. Gregory & Son, Marblehead, Mass.; Henderson, Peter Henderson & Co., New York, N. Y.; J. & S., Johnson & Stokes, Philadelphia, Penn.; Landreth, D. Landreth & Sons, Philadelphia, Penn.; N. K. & Co., Northrup,

King & Co., Minneapolis, Minn.; Salzer, John H. Salzer Seed Co., LaCrosse, Wis.; Vaughan, Vaughan's Seed Store, Chicago, Ill.

ABBREVIATIONS IN TABLES.

Ob., oblong; ov., oval; r., round; rs., roundish; l., light; d., dark; s., striped; g., green; br., broad; m., mottled; n., netted; y., yellow; sm., smooth.

Where nothing is stated concerning productiveness in the following descriptions and tables, it indicates that the variety was not satisfactorily productive.

In a few cases ripe specimens were obtained for the photographs, but subsequent field notes showed that the variety really belonged in a later class.

AMERICAN WATERMELONS, SEPTEMBER 16, 1899.

No.	NAME.	Seedsman.	Hills Planted.	Hills Grew.	Size of Fruit. Diameters in inches. Length	Bre'dth	Surface	Shape.	Maturity.	REMARKS.
1	American Queen	Landreth	6	6	7½	6½	l g	ov	Green	
2	Arkansas Traveler	Landreth	6	6	11½	5	l g s	ov	Green	
3	Black Boulder	J. & S.	6	6	8½	8	d g	ov	Almost ripe	Productive; flesh reddish
4	Black Diamond	J. & S.	6	6	7	7	d g	r	Almost ripe	
5	Black Spanish	Burpee	6	6	6½	6½	d g	r	Almost ripe	
6	The Boss	Burpee	6	6	12	6½	d g	ov	Turning	Medium productive
7	Bradford	Landreth	6	6	10½	6½	s	ov	Green	
8	Burpee's Cuban Queen	Burpee	6	6	7½	7	l g y	r	Green	Productive
9	Burpee's Mammoth Ironclad	Burpee	6	6	8½	6	l g	r	Green	
10	Burpee's White Gem	Burpee	6	6	7½	7	l g y	r	Turning	Productive
11	Citron Watermelon	Landreth	6	6	6	6½	l g br s	r	Flesh cream	Prod. for pres'ves; solid, heavy
12	City of Mexico	Salzer	6	6	7	8	d g	r	Turning	
13	Colorado Citron	Vaughan	6	6	6	6	lgbrdgs	r	Flesh cream	Prod. for preserves; very solid
14	Colorado Preserving Citron	Burpee	6	6	6¾	7	lgbrdgs	r	Flesh cream	Productive for preserves; solid
15	Cuban Queen	Landreth	6	4	6¾	6¾	d g s	r	Turning	
16	Cole's Early	Burpee	6	6	6½	6	d g s	rs	Turning	
17	Dark Green Rind Icing	Landreth	6	6	6¾	6¼	d g	r	Turning	
18	Dark Icing	Vaughan	6	6	7	6	d g	rs	Turning	
19	Dark Sweet Icing	J. & S.	6	6	8½	7	d g	ob	Turning	
20	Delaware	Burpee	6	6	7½	6	l g s	ob	Green	
21	Dixie	Burpee	6	6	5¾	5	l g s	r	Green	
23	Duke Jones	Burpee	6	6	8	6¾	d g s	r	Turning	
24	Excelsior	Landreth	6	6	7½	7	l g s	r	Turning	Productive
25	Extra Early	Landreth	6	6	9	6	l&d gm	ob	Turning	Productive
26	Ferry's Peerless	Gregory	6	6	6¼	5½	......	r	Green	
27	Florida Favorite	Burpee	6	5	7	5½	l g d m	ob	Turning	
28	Fordhook Early	Burpee	6	6	6	6	....	r	Turning	
29	Frame's Santiago	Burpee	6	6	8	5½	l g s	ob	Green	
30	Georgia	Landreth	6	6	7¾	7	l g s	ob	Turning	
31	Girardeau's New Favorite	Burpee	6	6	10	5½	g s	ob	Turning	
32	Glory of Asia	Salzer	6	6	6	6	d g	r	Turning	Productive
33	Golden Rind	Salzer	6	6	7½	6	y	rs	Turning	Productive
34	Gragg	Gregory	6	6	5½	5½	l g	r	Green	
35	Gray Monarch, or Long White	J. & S.	6	6	7½	6½	l g	rs	Turning	
36	Green and Gold	Burpee	6	6	6¾	6	dg m lg	rs	Turning	Flesh yellow
37	Green Citron	J. & S.	6	6	6¼	6	brlgdgs	r	Flesh cream	Productive for preserves

AMERICAN WATERMELONS, SEPTEMBER 16, 1899.

No.	NAME.	Seedsman.	Hills Planted.	Hills Grew.	Size of Fruit. Diameters in inches. Length	Bre'dth	Surface	Shape.	Maturity.	REMARKS.
38	Gypsy	Landreth	6	6	5½	5	l g s	r	Green	
39	Gypsy Rattlesnake	J. & S.	6	6	8¾	6	l g s	r	Turning	Productive
40	Hoosier King	Vaughan	6	5	8	6½	l g s	ob	Turning	
41	Honey	Gregory	6	6	6½	6	d g	rs	Turning	Productive
42	Hungarian Honey	Burpee	6	6	5½	5	d g	rs	Turning	
43	Icecream	Burpee	6	6	7	6	l g	ov	Turning	
44	Improved Black Spanish	J. & S.	6	6	7	7	black g	rs	Almost ripe	
45	Improved Kolb's Gem	Vaughan	6	6	6½	6¼	dg s	r	Turning	
46	Icing, or Ice Rind	Burpee	6	6	6	6¼	g	r	Turning	Productive
47	Indiana Sweetheart	Landreth	6	6	6½	6	l y g	r	Turning	
48	Jackson	Landreth	6	6	7	6½	l y g	rs	Green	
49	James River	Landreth	6	6	9½	5½	d g s	ov	Turning	
50	Johnson's Christmas	Salzer	6	6	5½	5½	dg s	r	Turning	
51	Johnson's Dixie	J. & S.	6	6	7½	6	l g b g s	rs	Turning	
52	Jones	Burpee	6	6	7½	6	l g	ob	Turning	
53	Jones' Jumbo	J. & S.	6	6	6½	6½	l g	r	Turning	
54	Jumbo	N., K. & Co.	6	5	5	5½	d g	rs	Green	
55	Kentucky Wonder	Burpee	6	6	10	6½	d g	ov	Turning	Productive
56	Kleckley Sweet	Burpee	6	6	10½	6	d g	ov	Turning	Productive
57	Kolb's Gem, or American Champion	Burpee	6	6	6	7	l g, g s	rs	Turning	Productive
58	Landreth's Boss	Landreth	6	6	11¾	6½	very d g	ov	Turning	
59	Landreth's Long Light Rind Icing	Landreth	6	6	7½	6½	very l g	ob	Turning	Productive
60	Light Green Rind Icing	Landreth	6	6	6½	7	very l g	rs	Ripe	Productive
61	Livingston's Nabob	Burpee	6	6	7	7	l & dgm	r	Turning	Productive
62	Long Dixie	Landreth	6	6	6½	5½	lgbrdgs	ov	Green	
63	Long White Icing	Vaughan	6	6	8½	7	l g	ov	Turning	
64	McIver's Wonderful Sugar	Burpee	6	6	8½	5¾	l g s	ov	Turning	
65	Mammoth Blue Gem	J. & S.	6	6	7	7	d g	r	Almost ripe	Productive
66	Mammoth Ironclad	J. & S.	6	4	7	4½	l g s	ov	Green	
67	Memphis	Henderson	6	6	10	5¾	l & d g s	ov	Green	
68	Mountain Sweet	J. & S.	6	6	10½	5½	d g	ov	Turning	
69	New Black-Eyed Susan	J. & S.	6	6	7½	6½	l & d g s	ov	Turning	
70	New Triumph	Burpee	6	6	6	6	d g s	r	Turning	
71	N. K. & Co.'s Kentucky Wonder	N. K. & Co.	6	6	8¾	5¾	l g	ov	Turning	
72	N. K. & Co.'s Klondike	N. K. & Co.	6	6	8	5½	l & d g s	ov	Almost ripe	Productive
73	Odella	Salzer	6	6	8¼	7¼	d & l g s	ov	Turning	

AMERICAN WATERMELONS, SEPTEMBER 16, 1899.

No.	NAME.	Seedsman.	Hills Planted.	Hills Grew.	Size of Fruit. Diameters in inches.		Surface	Shape.	Maturity.	REMARKS.
					Length	Bre'dth				
74	Orange	Gregory	6	6	8	6½	d g s	ov	Turning	....
75	Peerless	Landreth	6	6	9½	6¼	d g s	ov	Ripe	Productive
76	Phinney's Early Oval	Burpee	6	6	7½	6	l&d g m	ov	Turning	Productive
77	Phinney's Improved	Vaughan	6	6	9	6¼	l&d g m	ov	Ripe	Productive
78	Pride of Georgia	Burpee	6	6	8	7¼	l& d g s	rs	Ripe	....
79	Rattlesnake	Vaughan	6	6	7	6	l& d g s	ov	Turning	....
80	Red Seeded Citron	Vaughan	6	6	6½	7	l & d g	rs	Flesh cream	Very productive, for preserves
81	Red Seeded Vancluse	Burpee	6	6	9½	6	d g	ov	Almost ripe	Productive
82	Ruby Gold	Burpee	6	6	10	7	l g	ov	Turning	Flesh yellow
83	Salzer's Earliest	Salzer	6	6	8	7	l & d g s	rs	Almost ripe	Productive
84	Salzer's Fourth of July	Salzer	6	6	7½	6½	very d g	rs	Ripe	....
85	Salzer's Giant Sweet	Salzer	6	5	11½	6½	l g s	ov	Turning	....
86	Salzer's Oh, My!	Salzer	6	6	8½	8	d g s	rs	Almost ripe	....
87	Salzer's White Rind	Salzer	6	6	6½	6¼	l y g	r	Turning	....
88	Scaly Bark	J. & S.	6	6	6	5¾	l g	r	Green	....
89	Selected Johnson's Dixie	J. & S.	6	6	7½	5½	l g d g s	ob	Turning	....
90	Seminole	Burpee	6	4	11	5½	very l g	ob	Turning	....
91	Southern Rattlesnake	N. K. & Co.	6	6	12	6	l g s	ov	Turning	....
92	Stokes' Extra Early	J. & S.	6	6	5½	5	d g s	ov	Almost ripe	Productive; seeds very small
93	Striped Gypsy	Burpee	6	6	8	6¾	d g	ov	Turning	....
94	Sweet Siberian	Henderson	6	6	8	5	d g	ov	Turning	Flesh yellow
95	Sweetheart	Henderson	6	6	8	8	l g	r	Almost ripe	Productive
96	Triumph	J. & S.	6	6	7½	7	d g s	rs	Turning	Productive
97	True Ice Cream	Vaughan	6	6	8	5	d g	ov	Turning	Productive
98	Vick's Early	Burpee	6	6	9	5½	d g	ov	Turning	....
99	Volga	Henderson	6	6	7	7	l g	r	Turning	Productive
100	White Gem	J. & S.	6	0	....	....	....	....	....	....
101	Wisconsin Hydrid	Salzer	6	6	6	6½	d g s	rs	Turning	Productive
102	Wonderful Sugar	Salzer	6	6	9½	6	l g s	ov	Turning	....
103	Russian Mennonite No. 10	Windom, Minn.	6	0	....	....	....	....	....	....
104	Russian Mennonite No. 7	Windom, Minn.	6	5	6	5	l g	rs	Ripe	....
105	From Bokhara, Turkestan	(Per Rickmers)	6	6	9	7	g s	ov	Turning	Flesh yellow
106	From Samara, Russia	(Per Hansen)	6	6	8	7	very l g	rs	Green	Very productive

FOREIGN WATERMELONS, SEPTEMBER 16, 1899.

U. S. Dept. No.	NAME	Original Source.	Hills Planted.	Hills Grew.	Size of Fruit. Diameters in inches. Length	Bre'dth	Surface	Shape.	Maturity.	REMARKS.
16	From Belbek	Crimea, Russia	3	2	11	16	d g	ov	Almostripe	....
18	From Russia	Yokohoma, Japan	4	4	6¼	5	d g	rs	Turning	Productive; small seed
20	Favorite of the Pjatigorsk Farm	Russia	4	4	6½	6½	d g s	r	Almostripe	Productive
22	The Czar of Baktcha	Russia	4	4	6	5	l & d g s	ov	Turning	....
23	Favorite of the Pjatigorsk Farm	Russia	4	4	7	7	d g s	r	Fully ripe	Productive
24	Jea Teveam	China	4	4	10	6	d g	ob	Almostripe	Productive
25	Cream of Japan	Rnssia	4	4	8	6	d g s	ob	Almostripe	Productive; flesh light yellow
26	From Russia	Afghanistan	4	4	7½	6½	d g s	ob	Turning	Flesh yellow; productive
29	From Russia	Chimkent, Turk'n	4	4	7	7¼	l g s	r	Turning	....
32	From Russia	....	4	0	....	....	....	....	....	Too few seeds planted
33	Koula	Turkestan	4	4	7½	6¾	d g s	rs	Turning	Productive
35	From Russia	Khiva, Turkestan	4	3	6½	6¼	l g d g s	r	Turning	....
39	Striped Kamishine	Moscow, Russia	4	4	5½	5½	l g s	r	Green	Flesh yellow
40	Kaikalar Winter	Moscow, Russia	4	2	4	5	l g	r	Green	....
41	From Russia	Afghanistan	4	4	5	5½	l g	rs	Turning	Flesh yellow
43	Favorite of the Pjatigorsk Farm	Russia	4	1	6½	6½	d g s	r	Turning	Flesh yellow; productive
44	Caucasian	Russia	4	4	7½	7¼	v'y l g s	r	Turning	Productive
45	Theodosian	Russia	4	4	10½	6	d g s	r	Turning	Productive
46	White Crimean	Russia	4	4	9¾	6	d g m	ov	Turning	Productive
47	Kula	Rнssia	4	4	6	6	l g s	r	Turning	Productive
48	Pineapple	Russia	4	4	8	7	l g	rs	Turning	Productive
49	Incomparable	Russia	4	4	9	8	l g s	ob	Almostripe	Productive
50	Korean	Russia	4	3	10	5½	very l g	ov	Turning	Productive
55	From Russia	Shemakhinski	4	4	9	5½	d g s	ov	Turning	....
61	Raspberry Cream	Russia	4	4	15	6½	d g	ov	Almostripe	Productive
64	Pearl of Kishinev	Southwest Russia	4	4	7	6	l g s	rs	Turning	Flesh yellow; productive
69	Crimean	Crimea, Russia	4	4	6	6	l d g s	r	Green	Productive; two types
70	From Russia	Belbek, Russia	4	4	10¼	6½	d g	ov	Almostripe	Flesh yellow; productive
71	From Russia	Kashgar, Turk'tan	4	4	6	6	d g s	r	Turning	....
72	Incomparable	Russia	4	4	8	7	l g s	ob	Almostripe	Flesh yellow. productive
73	Khan	Khiva, Turkestan	4	3	7	6½	d g	rs	Turning	
75	Monastery	Russia	4	4	7	6½	d g s	rs	Turning	Productive
76	Aksa	Russia	4	4	7	6	l g	rs	Green	....
79	From Russia	Russia	4	3	10	6	very l g	ov	Ripe	....
80	Improved Black	Russia	4	4	8	7½	l g s	rs	Almostripe	Productive
82	Christmas Gift	Russia	4	3	6	6	d g	r	Green	

FOREIGN WATERMELONS, SEPTEMBER 16, 1899.

U.S. Dept. No.	NAME	Original Source	Hills Planted	Hills Grew	Size of Fruit. Diameters in inches.		Surface	Shape	Maturity	REMARKS
					Length	Bre'dth				
84	Kopanski	Russia	4	4	7	7½	d g	r	Turning	Productive
85	Cavenis	Khiva, Turk'stan	4	4	6	6¼	l & d g 8	r	Turning	
86	Afghanistan Pearl	Afghanistan	4	4	11	8	d g	ov	Turning	Flesh yellow
87	Cream of Japan	Russia	4	3	9	7	d g s	ob	Turning	
88	From Russia	Russia	4	4	7½	6¾	d g	rs	Turning	
89	Baikal	Russia	4	4	9½	7½	d g	ov	Turning	Flesh yellow
91	From South Ussurie	Eastern Siberia	4	4	6	5½	d g	rs	Turning	Productive
92	From Russia	Turkestan	4	4	9	5½	d g s	ov	Turning	Very productive
93	Roubanski Rjabko	Russia	4	4	7¼	7	l g s	ov	Turning	
91	Czar of Baktsha	Chimkent, T'kst'n	4	4	8	5½	l g s	rs	Turning	Type varies
102	From Russia	Russia	4	4	6½ 8 7	6 7 7	l g s	Varies	Ripe	Productive three; types
104	Pearl of Kishinev	Russia	4	4	9	6	d g s	ov	Ripe	
105	Favorite of the Pjatigorsk Farm	Afghanistan	4	4	8	6	d g	ov	Turning	Productive
106	From Russia	Turkestan	4	4	8¼	8	l g	r	Turning	
1193	From Samarkand	Turkestan	4	4	10¼	6	very l g	ov	Turning	Productive
1194	From Samarkand	Turkestan	4	2	3	3¼	l g	r	Very green	Too late

NOTES ON WATERMELONS, 1899.

The following varieties ripened fruit before the frost killed the vines September 16th. The following descriptions were made from the first ripe fruit of each variety:

No. 4. Black Diamond; J & S. Ripe September 13th; fruit oval, 8½ inches long, 7¼ inches in diameter, weight 6 lb. 2 oz. Surface slightly ribbed, black green, flesh light pink, seeds white tipped with black, flavor poor.

No. 25. Extra Early; Landreth. Ripe September 13th; fruit oblong, 7x6 inches, weight 3 lbs. 12 oz. Surface almost smooth, color green, mottled, flesh light pink, seeds white, black tipped, flavor very good. Productive.

No 28. Fordhook Early; Burpee. Ripe September 13th; fruit roundish, diameter 6x6¼ inches, weight 4 lb. 2 oz. Surface almost smooth, dark green, flesh red, seeds small and white, flavor good.

No. 36. Green and Gold; Burpee. Ripe September 13th; fruit roundish, 7½x7 inches, weight 5 lbs. 10 oz. Surface smooth, dark green, flesh saffron yellow, seeds black, flavor good.

No. 52 Jones; Burpee. Ripe September 13th; fruit oblong, 11½x8 inches, weight 10 lbs. 6 oz. Surface slightly ribbed, solid dark green, flesh rich pink, seeds white, flavor very good.

No. 60. Light Green Rind Icing; Landreth. Ripe September 6th; fruit roundish, 7x6½ inches, weight 6 lbs. 12 oz. Surface slightly ribbed, light green, slightly veined with dark green, flesh pale pink, seeds white, flavor fair. Productive.

No. 68. Mountain Sweet; J. & S. Ripe September 13th; fruit roundish to oval, 6½x6 inches, weight 4 lbs. 2 oz. Surface smooth, dark green, somewhat striped, flesh light pink almost white, seeds brown, flavor not very rich but good.

No. 75. Peerless; Landreth. Ripe September 6th; fruit oval, 8x6½ inches, weight 4 lbs. 11 oz. Surface smooth, light green veined with dark green, flesh pink, seeds white, flavor very good. Productive.

No. 76. Phinney's Early Oval; Burpee. Ripe Semptember 6th; fruit oval, 9½x6½ inches, weight 5 lbs. 11 oz. Surface smooth, light green, almost completely covered with dark green stripes, flesh dark pink, seeds white with black tips, flavor excellent. Productive.

No. 77. Phinney's Improved; Vaughan. Ripe September 13th; fruit round, 7x7 inches, weight 4 lbs. 4 oz. Surface smooth, green, mottled, flesh pink, seeds white, flavor good. Productive.

No. 78. Pride of Georgia; Burpee. Ripe September 6th; fruit roundish, 9½x7¾ inches, weight 9 lbs. Surface slightly ribbed, dark green with a darker green stripe, flesh pale pink, seeds white, black tips, flavor not very good.

No. 82. Ruby Gold; Burpee. Ripe September 13th; fruit round, 7x6¾ inches, weight 5 lbs. 10 oz. Surface smooth, slightly ribbed, dark green, flesh saffron yellow, flavor fair.

No. 84. Salzer's Fourth of July; Salzer. Ripe September 6; fruit roundish, 8½x7 inches, weight 6 lbs. 8 oz. Surface uneven and slightly ribbed, dark green, flesh pink, seeds black, flavor excellent.

No. 98. Vick's Early; Burpee. Ripe September 13; fruit oval, 8x7 inches, weight 6 lbs. 8 oz. Surface slightly ribbed, green, flesh pink to red, seeds black, flavor good.

No. 101. Wisconsin Hybrid; Salzer. Ripe September 13; fruit roundish, 6½x6¾ inches, weight 5 lbs. 11 oz. Surface smooth, light green with broad dark green stripes, flesh pink, seeds black mottled, flavor good. Productive.

No. 104. Russian Mennonite No. 7; from Windom, Minn. Ripe September 6; fruit roundish, 8x7¼ inches, weight 6 lbs. 10 oz. Surface smooth, light green, spotted with small russet spots, flesh pink, seeds small black, flavor fair.

U. S. Dept. of Agr. No. 18. From Russia; originally from Yokohoma, Japan. Ripe September 13; fruit roundish, 8x7¼ inches, weight 6 lbs. 8 oz. Surface smooth, dark green, flesh pink, seeds small and red, flavor excellent. Productive.

U. S. Dept. of Agr. No. 23. "Favorite of the Pjatigorsk Farm;" from Russia. Ripe August 24; fruit round, 7 inches long, 7 inches in diameter, weight 4 lbs. 4 oz; fruit smooth, rind thin, dark green with rather narrow almost black green stripes, flesh a rich pink shading to red, fine grained, sweet, seeds white with black tips, few and small, flavor excellent. Productive; the earliest variety tested.

Hills given special treatment yielded fruit 14 inches long and 13 inches in diameter and weighing 14 lbs. 8 oz. (See description of Plate 3).

U. S. Dept. of Agr. No. 72. "Incomparable;" from Russia. Ripe September 13; fruit oval to round, 7½x7½ inches, weight 6 lbs. Surface smooth, slightly uneven, light green, distinct narrow stripes, flesh reddish yellow, seeds black, flavor good. Productive.

U. S. Dept. Agr. No. 88. From Russia. Ripe September 13; fruit oval, 9 by 8 inches, weight 9 lbs. Surface smooth, dark green; flesh dark pink, seeds brown, flavor excellent.

U. S. Dept. Agr. No. 92. From Russia. Originally from Turkestan. Ripe September 13; fruit oblong 11½x6½ inches, weight 7 lbs. 3 oz. Surface smooth, light green almost completely covered with broad dark-green stripes; flesh pink, seeds light brown with black edges, flavor fair. Productive.

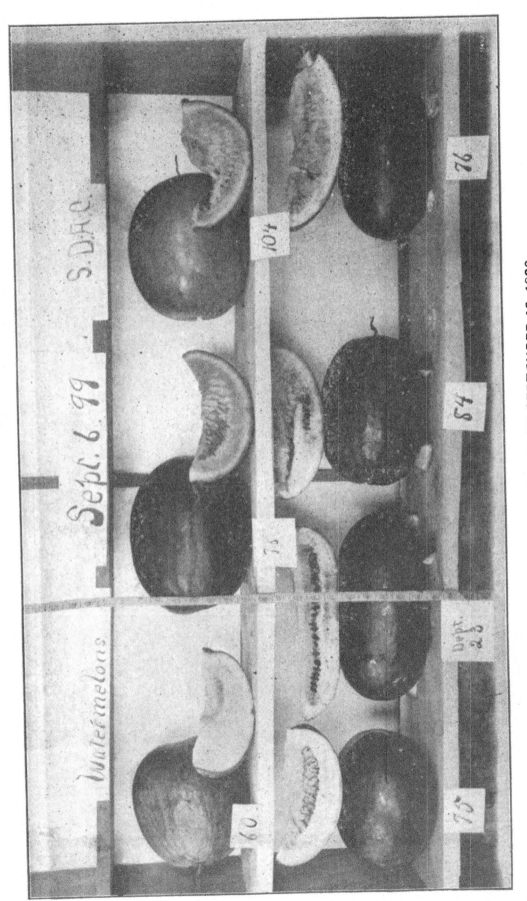

PLATE 1.—WATERMELONS, RIPE SEPTEMBER 16, 1899.

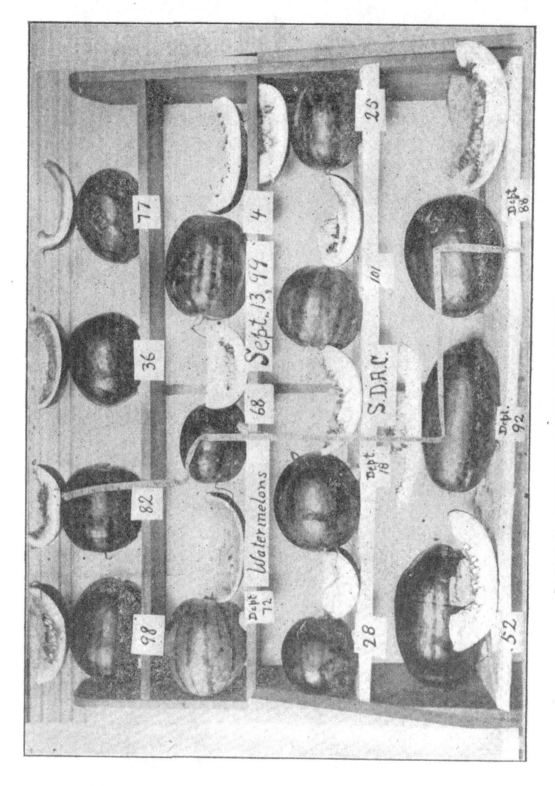

PLATE 2.—WATERMELONS, RIFE SEPTEMBER 13, 1899.

PLATE 3.—U. S. DEPT. OF AGR. No. 23. WATERMELONS.

SUMMARY OF WATERMELONS, 1899.

The varieties of watermelons ripe by September 6 are shown in Plate 1, viz.:

Upper row, beginning at the left side: No. 60, No. 78, No. 104.

Lower row: No. 75, Peerless; U. S. Dept. Agr. No. 23; No. 84, Salzer's Fourth of July; No. 76, Phinney's Early Oval.

Of these, Phinney's Early Oval and Salzer's Fourth of July were both early and of excellent quality. Of the others, Light Green Rind Icing and Peerless were the most producttive. U. S. Dept. No. 23 was the earliest variety and of excellent quality.

The varieties of watermelons ripe by September 13 are shown in Plate 2, viz.:

Upper row: No. 98, No. 82, No. 36, No. 77.
Second row: U. S. Dept. No. 72, No. 68, No. 4.
Third row: No. 28, U. S. Dept. No. 18, No. 101, No. 25.
Lower row: No. 52, U. S. Dept. No. 92, U. S. Dept. No. 88.

The following were both productive and of excellent or very good quality:

U. S. Dept. No. 18, No. 25, extra early.

Those both productive and of good quality were:

U. S. Dept. No. 72, Incomparable; No. 101, Wisconsin Hybrid; No. 77, Phinney's Improved; No. 68, Mountain Sweet.

U. S. Dept. No. 88 and No. 52, Jones, were larger than any of the above and ranked excellent or very good in quality, but lacked in productiveness. All these were red-fleshed except U. S. Dept. No. 72, which had reddish yellow flesh.

CITRONS.

Nos. 11, 13, 14, 37 and 80 were all citrons, used for preserves. All were productive.

AMERICAN MUSKMELONS, SEPTEMBER 16, 1899.

No.	NAME.	Seedsman.	Hills Planted.	Hills Grew.	Size of Fruit. Diameters in inches. Length	Bre'dth	Surface	Maturity. Sept. 16.	REMARKS.
1	Acme	Salzer	6	6	6	4½	g n	Green	Productive; not early enough
2	Acme Cantaloupe	Landreth	6	6	5½	4¾	y n	Ripe Sept 16	Productive; excellent quality
3	Acme, or Baltimore	Burpee	6	4	6¾	5½	g n	Ripe Sept 16	Too late
4	Anna Arundel	Landreth	6	6	7¼	5¼	g n	Ripe Sept 16	Productive; too late
112	Anna Arundel	J. & S.	7	7	7¾	5¼	g y n	Green	Productive; poor; too late
5	Atlantic City	Landreth	6	6	7	5¾	y g n	Ripe Sept 12	Productive
6	Banana	Burpee	6	6	14½	3¾	g sm	Ripe Sept 16	Productive; too late
111	Banquet	Burpee	7	7	4¾	4¾	g n	Ripe Sept 16	Productive; not early enough
8	Beck's Columbus	Burpee	7	4	6¾	5¾	n	Green	Too late
9	Boston Mango	Burpee	7	6	10	4¾	g n	Ripe Aug 29	Used for pickling; flesh yellow; too late
10	Bay View	Burpee	7	7	11½	6¾	g n	Ripe Sept 12	Very productive; a little too late
11	Burpee's Champion Market	Burpee	7	7	6¼	5	g n	Green	Productive; too late
12	Burpee's Golden Eagle	Burpee	7	7	6	4½	y g	Green	Productive; too late; yellow flesh
13	Burpee's Melrose	Burpee	7	7	5	4½	y g n	Ripe Sept 16	Productive; too late; excellent
14	Burpee's Netted Gem	Burpee	7	7	4½	3¾	y g	Ripe Sept 9	Productive; early enough
15	California Yellow Flesh	Landreth	7	7	6½	5¼	g n	Ripe Sept 16	Productive; too late
16	Cannon Ball	J. & S.	7	5	4¼	5	g n	Green	Too late
17	Cannon Ball	Burpee	7	6	5	4½	g n	Green	Too late
114	Captain	J. & S.	7	7	4¼	4¼	g n	Ripe Sept 8	Late; excellent
18	Carmes	Henderson	7	7	6½	7¾	g sm	Ripe Sept 16	Productive; large, but too late
19	Casaba Persian, or Ispahan	Landreth	7	7	10½	5½	y n	Ripe Sept 16	Large; not early; fairly productive
20	Champion Market	Gregory	7	7	5¼	5¼	g n	Green	Productive, but too late
21	Cantaloupe, Extra Early June	Landreth	7	6	5½	6	g n	Green	Too late
22	Champion Market	J. & S.	7	7	6¼	5¼	g n	Ripe Sept 12	Productive; early
23	Chicago Market	Burpee	7	6	8	7	g n	Ripe Sept 9	Productive; too late
24	Cosmopolitan	Burpee	7	7	6½	5½	g n	Green	Productive; too late
25	Cincinnati Market	Landreth	7	3	5¼	6	g n	Ripe Sept 16	Productive; too late
26	Columbus	Gregory	7	7	6	5¼	l g	Green	Too late
27	Delmonico	Burpee	7	7	7½	5¾	y n	Ripe Sept 16	Productive; not early; poor quality
28	Extra Early Grand Rapids	Burpee	7	7	7	6	g n	Ripe Sept 3	Productive; poor quality
29	Extra Early Citron, or Nutmeg	N. K. & Co.	7	6	5¾	5	g n	Ripe Sept 2	Early enough
30	Early Nutmeg	Burpee	7	7	6	6⅛	g n	Green	Productive; too late; poor quality
31	Early Netted Gem	N. K. & Co.	7	7	6½	5¼	g n	Ripe Sept 12	Productive; early; excellent
32	Emerald Gem	Burpee	7	7	5	5	d g sm	Ripe Sept 9	Productive; very early; excellent
33	Early Hackensack	Henderson	7	7	6	6	gray gn	Ripe Sept 16	Productive, but not early
34	Earliest Ripe	Salzer	7	6	4½	4½	d g sm	Ripe Sept 2	Early

AMERICAN MUSKMELONS, SEPTEMBER 16, 1899.

No.	NAME.	Seedsman.	Hills Planted.	Hills Grew.	Size of Fruit Diameters in inches. Length	Bre'dth	Surface	Maturity Sept. 16.	REMARKS.
35	Extra Early Prize	J. & S.	7	7	5	5	g n	Ripe Sept. 9	Productive, but rather late and small
36	Extra Early Hackensack	N. K. & Co.	7	7	5½	5¾	g n	Ripe Sept. 12	Too late
37	Extra Early Hackensack	J. & S.	7	7	5½	6¼	gray gn	Green	Productive; too late
38	Early Hackensack	Salzer	7	7	6	6¾	g n	Green	Productive; too late
39	Early Burlington	Landreth	7	7	6	5	g n	Ripe Sept. 16	Productive
40	Early Bristol	Landreth	7	7	5	6	g n	Ripe Sept. 9	Productive; not early
41	Extra Early Cape May	Landreth	7	7	5½	5¾	g n	Green	Productive; too late
42	Extra Early	Landreth	7	3	4¾	4½	y g n	Ripe Sept. 16	Productive; not early
43	Giant of Colorado	J. & S.	7	6	11	4¾	g n	Ripe Sept. 16	Late
44	Green Fleshed Osage	Burpee	7	7	6½	4½	g sm	Green	Productive; too late
45	Golden Netted	Gregory	7	7	5½	4	g n	Ripe Sept. 16	Productive; early
46	Green	Landreth	7	7	6	5	g sm	Ripe Sept. 2	Not productive
47	Golden Jenny	Landreth	7	7	6	4¼	g n	Ripe Sept. 8	Excellent; not early
48	Hackensack, or Turk's Cap	Burpee	7	7	7½	6½	g n	Green	Productive; too late
49	Ivy Gem	J. & S.	7	7	6½	6¼	g sm	Green	Very productive; not early
50	Improved Christiana	Henderson	7	7	5¼	5½	g sm	Ripe Sept. 16	Productive
51	Improved Jenny	Landreth	7	7	4	4½	g n	Ripe Sept. 16	Productive
52	Iron Clad	Burpee	7	7	6½	5½	g n	Ripe Sept. 16	Productive, but too late
53	McCleary's Improved Jenny Lind	J. & S.	7	7	3½	4	g n	Ripe Sept. 9	Very productive; not early
54	Jenny Lind	Landreth	7	7	4	4¾	g n	Ripe Sept. 4	Productive; early enough
55	Jersey Belle	Burpee	7	7	4	5	g n	Ripe Sept. 8	Productive, but late
56	Kinsman Queen	Burpee	7	7	5½	5¾	g sm	Green	Productive; yellow flesh
57	Large Acme	Landreth	7	7	7	6	g n	Green	Productive; too late
58	Large Black Paris	Landreth	7	7	8½	7½	g n	Green	Productive; too late
59	Large White French	Landreth	7	7	8	6¼	g sm	Green	Productive; too late
113	Lone Star	J. & S.	7	7	6¼	5¾	l g sm	Green	Too late
60	Long Island Beauty	Burpee	7	7	5	5¾	g n	Ripe Sept. 16	Productive
61	Montreal Green Nutmeg	Burpee	7	6	7	6	g n	Ripe Sept. 16	Productive; excellent; not early
62	Montreal Improved Nutmeg	J. & S.	7	7	6¼	7¼	g n	Ripe Sept. 12	Very productive, but not early
63	Montreal Market	Henderson	7	7	6½	7	g n	Green	Productive; too late
64	Montreal Nutmeg	Gregory	7	6	7	6½	g n	Green	Productive; too late
65	Missouri	Landreth	7	7	4½	5½	g n	Green	Too late
66	Montreal	Landreth	7	7	5½	6¼	g n	Green	Productive; too late
67	Melrose	Vaughan	7	7	5	4½	g n	Ripe Sept. 16	Productive; not early
68	New Superior	Burpee	7	7	5	5¼	g n	Ripe Sept. 12	Productive; not early enough
69	New Early Hackensack	Burpee	7	7	6	6¼	g n	Ripe Sept. 9	Productive, but not early

AMERICAN MUSKMELONS, SEPTEMBER 16, 1899.

No.	NAME.	Seedsman.	Hills Planted.	Hills Grew.	Size of Fruit Diameters in inches.		Surface	Maturity Sept. 16.	REMARKS.
					Length	Bre'dth			
70	New Green Fleshed	J. & S.	7	6	6¼	5	g n	Green	Productive; too late
71	New Grand Rapids	J. & S.	7	7	7¾	7¼	y g n	Ripe Sept. 6	Productive, but not early enough
72	New Melrose	J. & S.	7	7	4¾	4½	g n	Ripe Sept. 12	Productive; not early
73	Newport	Henderson	7	7	3¼	4¾	g n	Ripe Sept. 9	Productive. early
74	New Osage	J. & S.	7	7	7	5	g n	Green	Not early enough; yellow flesh
75	Nutmeg	Henderson	7	7	6¼	5½	y g n	Ripe Sept. 12	Productive; early
76	Netted Beauty	J. & S.	7	7	4½	5	d g n	Ripe Sept. 16	Productive; not early enough
77	Netted Gem	Henderson	7	7	5½	5	g n	Green	Productive; very good quality
78	Netted Gem	Landreth	7	7	5¼	4	g n	Ripe Sept. 9	Productive, but late
79	Netted Nutmeg	Landreth	7	7	6¼	4¾	g n	Ripe Sept. 12	Very productive and early
80	N. K. & Co.'s California Cream	N. K. & Co.	7	7	6	6½	g n	Ripe Sept. 9	Productive, but late
81	N. K. & Co.'s Yellow Meated Japan	N. K. & Co.	7	7	7¼	6	g n	Green	Productive; too late; flesh yellow
82	Osage	Landreth	7	7	7½	6	g n	Green	Productive; too late; flesh yellow
83	Osage	Salzer	7	7	5¾	4¾	g n	Green	Productive; too late; flesh yellow
84	Osage, or Miller Cream	Burpee	7	7	6¼	5½	g sm	Creen	Productive; too late; flesh yellow
141	Osage Select	Vaughan	7	7	6	5	g n	Green	Very productive; too late; flesh yellow
85	Paul Rose, or Petoskey	Burpee	7	7	5¼	4¼	g n	Ripe Sept. 16	Productive
86	Paul Rose	J. & S.	7	7	4½	3½	g n	Ripe Sept. 16	Productive
87	Paul Rose	Henderson	7	7	5¼	4½	g n	Ripe Sept. 16	Productive
88	Perfected Delmonico	Burpee	7	7	5½	6½	y n	Green	Productive; too late; flesh yellow
89	Perfection	Burpee	7	7	7	6½	g n	Ripe Sept. 16	Productive
90	Persian Monarch	J. & S.	7	7	4	4¾	lg m dg	Green	Flesh yellow; too late
91	Pineapple	Landreth	7	7	6	5½	g n	Ripe Sept. 16	Productive; too late
92	Pineapple	Salzer	7	7	9½	6	g n	Ripe Sept. 16	Productive; too late
93	Princess	J. & S.	7	7	8	6	g n	Green	Productive; flesh yellow; too late, poor
94	Prolific Nutmeg	Burpee	7	7	5	4¾	y n	Ripe Sept. 9	Productive; early
95	Queen of All	Salzer	7	7	6¼	5	d g sm	Green	Productive; too late; flesh yellow
96	Reedland Giant	Landreth	7	7	10	4¾	g n	Ripe Sept. 16	Productive; too late
97	Reedland Giant	Burpee	7	7	9	4½	y n	Ripe Sept. 16	Productive; too late
98	Rocky Ford	Landreth	7	7	4½	3¼	g y n	Ripe Sept. 8	Productive; good
99	Rocky Ford	Henderson	7	7	5	4¾	g n	Ripe Sept. 12	Very productive; excellent; flesh green
101	Rocky Ford	J. & S.	7	7	4	3½	g n	Ripe Sept. 9	Productive; early; excellent
102	Shumway's Giant	N. K. & Co.	7	7	6	7¼	l g sm	Ripe Sept. 9	Productive; too late
103	Six Oaks	Landreth	7	7	5½	5½	g y n	Ripe Sept. 9	Not early
104	South Jersey	Landreth	7	7	7	5½	g n	Green	Productive; too late
105	Skillman's Netted	Henderson	7	7	5½	5¾	g y	Ripe Sept. 16	Productive; too late

AMERICAN MUSKMELONS, SEPTEMBER 16, 1899.

No.	NAME.	Seedsman.	Hills Planted.	Hills Grew.	Size of Fruit Diameters in inches: Length	Bre'dth	Surface	Maturity Sept. 16.	REMARKS.
115	Shipper's Delight	J. & S.	7	7	6¼	6¼	g n	Ripe Sept. 8	Productive; very small, flesh green, ex.
106	Superb	Burpee	7	7	6	6¼	g n	Ripe Sept. 9	Productive; too late
107	Salmon and Green	Landreth	7	7	6½	5¼	d g sm	Green	Productive; too late, flesh green
108	Salzer's Nectar of Angels	Salzer	7	7	7½	6½	g n	Ripe Sept. 2	Productive; early enough
109	Shumway's Giant	Gregory	7	7	6	7¾	g sm	Green	Productive; too late, thick flesh
110	Surprise	Burpee	7	7	7	6¾	g sm	Green	Productive; too late, flesh yellow
116	Togoodo Spanish Winter	J. & S.	7	7	8	5¼	d g sm	Green	Flesh green, too late
117	Tip Top Nutmeg	Burpee	7	7	7¾	6½	l g sm	Green	Too late
118	Triumph	Burpee	7	7	7½	6	l g n	Green	Too late
119	Ward's Nectar	J. & S.	7	7	4¼	4¾	d g n	Ripe Sept. 16	Productive; too late
120	White Japan	Burpee	7	7	5	5	g n	Green	Productive: too late, flesh green
121	Russian Mennonite No. 1	Windom, Minn	7	5	7¼	6	y n	Ripe Sept. 12	Productive; flesh yellow, poor quality
122	Russian Mennonite No. 2-	Windom, Minn	7	7	8½	6	g y n	Ripe Sept. 6	Productive; too late
123	Russian Mennonite No. 3	Windom, Minn	7	3	4	3	g sm	Green	Much too late
124	Russian Mennonite No. 4	Windom, Minn	7	5	9½	6¾	g sm	Ripe Aug. 29	
125	Russian Mennonite No. 5	Windom, Minn	7	4	4	4½	g sm	Green	Too late
126	Southern Beauty	Vaughan	7	6	8	5½	g n	Green	Productive; too late
127	Extra Early Giant Prolific	Vaughan	7	7	5¾	6¾	g n	Ripe Sept. 16	Productive; too late
128	Superior	Vaughan	7	7	5	5	g n	Ripe Sept. 16	Too late
129	Irondequoit	Vaughan	7	7	6	6¼	g n	Ripe Sept. 16	Productive; too late
130	The Newport	Vaughan	7	7	3¼	4½	g n	Ripe Sept. 16	Productive, excellent, early, flesh green
131	Vaughan's Select True Jenny Lind	Vaughan	7	7	8	5⅝	g n	Ripe Sept. 6	Productive; but late
132	Thorburn's Giant	Vaughan	7	7	5	7½	l g sm	Ripe Sept. 9	Productive; too late
133	Oval Netted Gem	Vaughan	7	7	4¾	4	g n	Ripe Sept. 12	Very productive; early
134	Grand Rapids	Vaughan	7	7	5¾	5½	g n	Ripe Sept. 6	Too late
135	New Orleans Market	Vaughan	7	7	6	6¼	g y n	Ripe Sept. 16	Productive
136	Chicago Market Ordinary	Vaughan	7	7	6	6¾	g n	Ripe Sept. 16	Productive; not early
137	Baltimore Acme	Vaughan	7	7	6¼	4½	g n	Green	Productive; too late, flesh green
138	Montreal Market Nutmeg	Vaughan	7	7	7	7	g n	Green	Productive; too late
139	Tip Top	Vaughan	7	7	6¼	5½	g n	Green	Productive; too late, flesh yellow
140	Round Netted Gem	Vaughan	7	7	5	4¼	g y n	Ripe Sept. 6	Productive; one of the earliest
142	Improved Cantaloupe	Vaughan	7	7	5	5¾	y g n	Ripe Sept. 12	Productive; fairly early
143	Giant Chicago Market	Vaughan	7	7	6¼	7¾	y g n	Ripe Sept. 16	Productive; too late
144	Melon Peach	Vaughan	6	6	3	3	y	Ripe Aug. 31	Very productive
145	Climbing Orange	Salzer	6	7	3	3	y	Ripe Sept. 2	Very productive
146	Vegetable Orange or Mango Melon	Salzer	6	6	3	3	y	Ripe Sept. 2	Very productive

AMERICAN MUSKMELONS, SEPTEMBER 16, 1899.

No.	NAME	Seedsman	Hills Planted.	Hills Grew.	Size of Fruit Diameters in Inches		Surface	Maturity Sept. 16.	REMARKS.
					Length	Bre'dth			
147	Pomegranate	Salzer	6	6	2¾	2¾	y d s	Ripe Sept. 2	Very productive
148	Vegetable Orange or Mango Melon	J. & S.	6	6	3	3	y	Ripe Sept. 2	Very productive
149	Melon Peach or Vegetable Orange	N. K. & Co.	6	6	3	3	y	Ripe Sept. 2	Very productive
156	Ornamental Pomegranate	Burpee	6	6	2¾	2¾	y d s	Ripe Sept. 2	Very productive

FOREIGN MUSKMELONS, 1899.

U. S. Dept. No.	NAME	Original Source	Hills Planted	Hills Grew	Size of Fruit Diameters in inches: Length	Bred'th	Surface	Maturity	REMARKS
	Zambitcha (a)	Bokhara	2	1	4½	3¾		Green	
	Kokand	Bokhara	2	1					No fruit
	Beckak	Bokhara	2	1					No fruit
	Andalack	Bokhara	2	2	3	1¼		Green	Fruit just forming
	Name Lost	Bokhara	2	1					No fruit
	Akkaoum (white)	Bokhara	2	1					No fruit
	Kourgatch	Bokhara	2	2	3½	2½		Green	Fruit just forming
	Zambitcha (b)	Bokhara	2	3	5	2½		Green	Fruit just forming
15	Kochanka	Russia	3	3	5¼	3½	g s	Ripe Sept. 9	Used for preserves
17	Empress of Melons	Russia	3	1	5½	5	g	Green	Too late; productive
19	Lenkoran No. 2	Transcaucasia	3	1	4½	3	g	Green	Too late
21	Gen. Skobeleff II	Khiva, Turkestan	3	3	5½	4½	l y	Green	Too late; productive
27	Mlle. Maroussia Lessevitzky	Russia	3	3	6	5	g	Ripe Sept. 12	Too late; productive
28	Kochanka	Russia	3	2	5	4½	g	Ripe Sept. 8	Too late
30	Mme. Lydia Lessevitzky	Russia	3	3	4½	5½	y	Ripe Sept. 16	Too late
31	Kook-kala-poosh	Bokhara	3	2					No fruit
34	Okh-Took	Bokhara	3	1					No fruit
36		Turkestan	3	1					No fruit
38	The Queen	Moscow, Russia	3	3	8½	7	g	Green	Too late; strong vine
42	Apricot	Moscow, Russia	3	3	5½	5½	g	Ripe Sept. 16	Too late
51	Kook-kala-poosh	Turkestan	3	1					No fruit
52	Queen of Muskmelons	Moscow, Russia	3	3	6	5	g	Ripe Sept. 16	Too late
53	Peach	Moscow, Russia	3	1	7	5	g	Green	Too late
54		Moscow, Russia	3	2	7	5¼	g	Green	Too late
56	Ukraine Pineapple	Southern Russia	3	3	5	5	g	Green	Too late
57	Ankelin	Vernoe, Turkestan	3	2	5	5½	g	Ripe Sept. 16	Too late
58	Osma	Moscow, Russia	3	3	8	4½	y g	Ripe Sept. 16	Too late
59	Lenkoran II	Transcaucasia	3	3	10	4½	g	Green	Too late
60	Lenkoran I	Transcaucasia	3	2	3½	1¾	g	Green	Too late
62	Getman's	Moscow, Russia	3	3	8	5½	g	Green	Too late
63	Reticulated Muskmelon	Moscow, Russia	3	2	8½	6	g	Green	Too late; flesh yellow
66	Lida	Crimea, Russia	3	3	4½	4½	g	Ripe Sept. 16	Too late
67	Petro Alexandrovski	Turkestan	3	2	4	2¼	g	Green	Too late
74		Moscow, Russia	3	3	6¼	5½	g	Green	Flesh thick, greenish white; too late
77	Crimean White	Crimea, Russia	3	1	6½	3¾	g	Green	Too late
81	Dubook (Oak)	Moscow, Russia	3	1	6	3½	g	Green	Too late

FOREIGN MUSKMELONS, 1899.

U.S. Dept. No.	NAME	Original Source	Hills Planted	Hills Grew	Size of Fruit Diameters in inches		Surface	Maturity	REMARKS
					Length	Br'dth			
95	Duijma	Khiva, Turkestan	3	1	2½	1	g	Green	Fruit forming; too late
96	Petschatka	Moscow, Russia	3	1	5	5½	g	Green	Too late
97	Marusja	Moscow, Russia	3	2	6½	4	d g	Green	Too late
98	President Akhsharoumov	Turkestan	3	3	10	5	d g	Green	Too late; productive
99	Petro-Alexandrovskian	Moscow, Russia	3	2	4¾	3½	d g s	Green	Too late
100	Gen. Scobeleff II	Khiva, Turkestan	3	1	4	4	l y	Almost Ripe	Yellow flesh; productive
101	Okh-oo-took	Moscow, Russia	3	1					No fruit
109	Woshtchanka	Moscow, Russia	3	2	5¼	4¼	l y	Green	Too late
114		Amu Daria, Turk.	1	1	3½	1¼		Green	Too late
120		Old Bokhara, Turk.	1	1	4	2		Green	Too late
1212	Ak-ka-in	Tashkend, R. Turk	2	1					No fruit
1214	Akitschick	Tashkend, R. Turk	3	2	3½	1½		Green	Much too late
1216		Tashkend, R. Turk	2	1	4½	4	g	Very Green	Much too late
1217	Kasak	Tashkend, R. Turk	2	1	3½	3¾		Very Green	Much too late
1218	Tschirin Beschek	China	2	1	7	3	d g	Green	Too late
1219	Kol-cash	Tashkend, R. Turk	3	1	3½	1½		Very Green	Too late
1225	Ak-ka-yur	Tashkend, R. Turk	3	1	9	4½	g	Green	Too late

From one to five hills were planted of each of the following varieties of muskmelons from which no results were obtained; the seed either failed to germinate or the vines were destroyed by insects: U. S. Dept. Agr. Nos. 4, 37, 78, 103, 107, 110, 115, 116, 117, 118, 119, 121, 122, 123, 836, 877, 1186, 1188, 1191, 1196, 1197, 1198, 1199, 1201, 1202, 1208, 1215, 1221, 1222, 1223, 1224, 1226, all Turkestan varieties.

NOTES ON MUSKMELONS, 1899.

No. 3. Acme or Baltimore. Burpee. Ripe September 16th; fruit round, 4½ inches long, 4½ inches broad, weight 1 lb. 13 oz. Skin greenish, much netted, flesh reddish, green next to the skin, poor. Neither productive nor early.

No. 4. Anna Arundel. Landreth. Ripe September 16th; fruit oval, 7x5½ inches, weight 3 lbs. 14 oz. Surface greenish yellow, much netted, flesh greenish white, very good. Productive but late.

No. 5. Atlantic City. Landreth. Ripe September 12th; fruit oval, 6x4½ inches, weight 2 lbs. 5 oz. Surface yellow, netted, flesh greenish white, very good. Productive.

No. 6. Banana. Burpee. Ripe September 16th; fruit very long, slender, 13½x3¼ inches. Skin smooth and yellow, flesh yellow, rather poor. Productive but late.

No. 9. Boston Mango. Burpee. Ripe August 29th; fruit oval, 8½x5 inches, weight 2 lbs. 4 oz. Skin yellow, netted, flesh pale yellow, lacking flavor and quality. Neither productive nor early; used for pickling.

No. 10. Bay View. Burpee. Ripe September 12th; fruit oval, 9x4½ inches, weight 3 lbs. 7 oz. Skin yellow, smooth, flesh greenish white, poor, very productive but a little late.

No. 14. Burpee's Netted Gem; Burpee. Ripe September 9th; fruit oval, 3¾x3¾ inches, weight 14 oz. Skin yellowish green, netted, flesh greenish, excellent. Productive and early.

No. 15. California Yellow Flesh. Landreth. Ripe September 16th; fruit roundish, 4½x4¾ inches, weight 2 lbs. 4 oz. Skin green with dark green netting, flesh orange yellow, fair. Productive.

No. 18. Carmes. Henderson. Ripe September 16th;

fruit oval, 6x5½ inches, weight 3 lbs. Skin greenish yellow, netted, flesh white, fairly good. Productive but too late.

No. 19. Casaba, Persian or Ispahan. Landreth. Ripe September 16th; fruit oval, pointed, 8¾x4½, weight 2 lbs. 11 oz. Skin yellow, smooth, a trace of netting, flesh yellowish white, poor. Fairly productive, but not early.

No. 22. Champion Market. J. & S. Ripe September 12th; fruit oval to round, 5¾x5½ inches, weight 3 lbs. 4 oz. Skin yellow, netted, flesh white, good. Productive, early.

No. 23. Chicago Market. Burpee. Ripe September 9th; fruit oval, 8x7 inches, weight 6 lbs. Skin green, netted, flavor excellent. Productive but late.

No. 27. Delmonico. Burpee. Ripe September 16th; fruit oval, 5½x4 inches, weight 2 lbs. 3 oz. Skin yellow, netted, flesh reddish yellow, poor. Productive but not early.

No. 28. Extra Early Grand Rapids. Burpee. Ripe September 3d; fruit oval, 7x5¾ inches, weight 3 lbs. 8 oz. Skin yellow, netted, flesh salmon yellow, poor quality. Productive.

No. 29. Extra Early Citron or Nutmeg. N. K. & Co. Ripe September 2d; fruit roundish, slightly oval, 3½x5½ inches, weight 1 lb. 8 oz. Skin yellowish green, somewhat netted, flesh light green, excellent. Early.

No. 31. Early Netted Gem. N. K. & Co. Ripe September 12th; fruit roundish, 3¾x4¼ inches, weight 1 lb. 9 oz. Skin greenish yellow, much netted, flesh greenish, having a peculiar spicy flavor, excellent. Productive and early.

No. 32. Emerald Gem. Burpee. Ripe September 9th; fruit roundish, 4½x5¼ inches, weight 2 lbs. 2 oz. Skin greenish yellow, netted, flesh yellow, excellent. Productive and very early.

No. 33. Early Hackensack. Peter Henderson. Ripe September 16th; fruit roundish, 5½x5¼ inches, weight 3 lbs. 1 oz. Skin yellow, netted, flesh yellowish white, poor, productive but not early.

No. 34. Earliest Ripe. Salzer. Ripe September 2d; fruit round, 4½x4½ inches, weight 1 lb. 13 oz. Skin greenish yellow, somewhat netted, flesh light green, good, early.

No. 35. Extra Early Prize. J. & S. Ripe September 9th; fruit oblate, 2x3¾ inches, weight 8 oz. Skin greenish yellow, flesh greenish, very good, productive, but rather late and small. Belongs rather in Plate 7.

No. 36. Extra Early Hackensack. N. K. & Co. Ripe September 12th; fruit roundish oblate, 3½x4¼ inches, weight 1 lb. 7 oz. Skin green, netted, flesh greenish, good. Too late.

No. 39. Early Burlington. Landreth. Ripe September 16th; fruit round, 5½x5 inches, weight 2 lbs. 5 oz. Skin yellowish green, netted, flesh light green, fairly good, later specimens were excellent. Productive.

No. 40. Early Bristol. Landreth. Ripe September 9th; fruit roundish, 4½x5 inches, weight 2 lbs. 8 oz. Skin covered with netting, flesh greenish, excellent flavor. Productive but not early.

No. 42. Extra Early. Landreth. Ripe September 2d; fruit roundish, 4¼x5½ inches, weight 2 lbs. 4 oz. Skin greenish yellow, netted, flesh greenish white, fairly good. Productive but not early.

No. 43. Giant of Colorado. J. & S. Ripe September 16th; fruit oval, 8x5 inches, weight 1 lb. 12 oz. Skin dark green, slightly netted, flesh greenish, poor. Late.

No. 45. Golden Netted. Gregory. Ripe September 16th; fruit roundish oval, 4½x3¾ inches, weight 1 lb. 6 oz. Skin yellowish green, netted, flesh greenish, excellent. Productive and early.

No. 46. Green. Landreth. Ripe September 2d; fruit

round oblate, 4½x5 inches, weight 1 lb. 12 oz. Skin greenish, netted, flesh light almost white, lacks quality.

No. 47. Golden Jenny. Landreth. Ripe September 8th; fruit round, 4½x4½ inches, weight 1 lb. 10 oz. Skin yellow, much netted, flesh greenish, very good to excellent, but not early.

No. 50. Improved Christiana. Henderson. Ripe September 16th; fruit roundish oblate, 4½x5½ inches, weight 2 lbs. 10 oz. Skin dark green, slightly netted, flesh reddish yellow, green next to the skin, fairly good. Productive.

No. 51. Improved Jenny. Landreth. Ripe September 16th; fruit oblate, 2½x4¼ inches, weight 1 lb. Skin greenish, netted, flesh greenish, excellent. Productive.

No. 52. Iron Clad. Burpee. Ripe September 16th; fruit roundish, 4¾x5 inches, weight 2 lbs. 4 oz. Skin yellow with very coarse open netting, flesh orange yellow, poor. Productive but late.

No. 53. McCleary's Improved Jenny Lind. J. & S. Ripe September 9th; fruit oblate, 2¾x4½ inches, weight 1 lb. Skin greenish yellow, covered with netting, flesh greenish, excellent. Very productive.

No. 54. Jenny Lind. Landreth. Ripe September 2d; fruit round oblate, 2½x4½ inches, weight 14 oz. Skin greenish, much netted, flesh greenish, excellent. Productive. This is the leader in quality of the early sorts.

No. 55. Jersey Belle. Burpee. Ripe September 8th; fruit roundish oblong, 4½x4 inches, weight 1 lb. 12 oz. Skin yellowish, covered with netting, flesh greenish, poor. Productive but late.

No. 60. Long Island Beauty. Burpee. Ripe September 16th; fruit roundish, 5½x6 inches, weight 3 lbs. 15 oz. Skin greenish yellow, wholly covered with netting, flesh greenish white, poor. Productive.

No. 62. Montreal Improved Nutmeg. J. & S. Ripe

September 12th; fruit roundish, 5½x5¼ inches, weight 4 lbs. Skin green almost wholly covered with netting, flesh greenish white, excellent. Very productive, not early.

No. 67. Melrose. Vaughan. Ripe September 12th; fruit oval, 6x5 inches, weight 2 lbs. 3 oz. Skin greenish, netted, flesh greenish, good. Productive but not early.

No. 69. New Early Hackensack. Burpee. Ripe September 9th; fruit roundish flat, 3½x4½ inches, weight 1 lb. 9 oz. Skin greenish, yellow netted, flesh greenish, excellent. Productive but not early.

No. 71. New Grand Rapids. J. & S. Ripe September 6th; fruit oblong, 7¾x6½ inches, weight 4 lbs., 14 oz. Skin yellow, somewhat netted, flesh reddish yellow, poor. Productive, but not early.

No. 72. New Melrose. J. & S. Ripe September 12th; fruit roundish oblate, 4½x5¾ inches, weight 3 lbs., 3 oz. Skin greenish yellow, obscurely ribbed and wholly covered with green netting, flesh greenish white, excellent. Productive, but not early.

No. 73. Newport. J. & S. Ripe September 9th; fruit oblate, 3x4¼ inches, weight 1 lb., 2 oz. Skin yellowish green, flesh green, excellent. Productive and matures early.

No. 75. Nutmeg. Henderson. Ripe September 12th; fruit round, 3¼x3¼ inches, weight 1 lb. Skin greenish yellow, slightly netted, flesh white tinged with green, excellent. Productive and early.

No. 76. Netted Beauty. J. & S. Ripe September 16; fruit roundish, 4½x4 inches, weight 1 lb 5 oz. Skin greenish yellow, netted, flesh greenish white, poor. Productive but not early enough.

No. 78. Netted Gem. Landreth. Ripe September 9th; fruit oval, 4x3¾ inches, weight 1 lb 2 oz. Skin yellowish, somewhat netted, flesh greenish white, good quality. Productive but late.

No. 79. Netted Nutmeg. Landreth. Ripe September 12; fruit oval, 6½x5 inches, weight 2 lbs 11 oz. Skin green, netted, flesh light green, good. Very productive and early.

No. 80. N. K. & Co.'s California Cream. N. K. & Co. Ripe September 9; fruit oblate, 5¼x6 inches, weight 3 lbs. 8 oz. Skin greenish yellow, covered with netting, flesh reddish yellow, excellent. Productive but late.

No. 85. Paul Rose, or Petovskey. Burpee. Ripe September 16th; fruit roundish, 3¾x3½ inches, weight 15 oz. Skin dark green, faintly netted, flesh orange yellow, very good. Productive.

No. 86. Paul Rose. J. & S. Ripe September 16th; fruit oval to round, 5x3¾ inches, weight 1 lb. 2 oz. Skin dark green, netted, flesh yellow, very good. Productive.

No. 87. Paul Rose. Henderson. Ripe September 16th; fruit roundish, 4x3¾ inches, weight 1 lb. 4 oz. Skin greenish yellow, flesh orange yellow, a peculiar spicy flavor, good. Productive.

No. 89. Perfection. Burpee. Ripe September 16th; fruit roundish, 5¼x5¾ inches, weight 3 lbs. 9 oz. Skin yellowish green, much netted, flesh deep orange yellow, sweet, very good. Productive.

No. 92. Pineapple. Salzer. Ripe September 16th; fruit oval, 6¼x5½ inches, weight 3 lbs. 5 oz. Skin yellowish, netted, flesh greenish white, very good. Productive. Too late.

No. 94. Prolific Nutmeg. Burpee. Ripe September 9th; fruit roundish to oblong, 5x4¾ inches, weight 1 lb. 4 oz. Skin greenish yellow, netted, flesh yellow, excellent. Productive and early.

No. 96. Reedland Giant. Landreth. Ripe September 16th; fruit roundish, 3½x4¼ inches, weight 1 lb. 5 oz. Skin greenish yellow, netted, flesh greenish white, poor. Productive but late.

No. 97. Reedland Giant. Burpee. Ripe September 16th; fruit long oval pointed, 9½x4½ inches, weight 3 lbs. 3 oz. Skin greenish yellow, slightly netted, flesh greenish white, fair. Productive but too late.

No. 98. Rocky Ford. Landreth. Ripe September 8th; fruit oblong, 4½x3¼ inches, weight 13 oz. Skin bright yellow, covered with netting, flesh green, good. Productive.

No. 99. Rocky Ford. Henderson. Ripe September 12th; fruit oval, 5x4¾ inches, weight 1 lb. 6 oz. Skin yellowish green, netted, flesh green, excellent. Very productive, early.

No. 101. Rocky Ford. J. & S. Ripe September 9th; fruit oblong, 4x3¾ inches, weight 1 lb. Skin dark green, covered with netting, flesh greenish, excellent. Productive and early.

No. 102. Shumway's Giant. N. K. & Co. Ripe September 9th; fruit roundish oblate, 6x7¾ inches, weight 5 lbs. 8 oz. Skin light yellow, nearly smooth, flesh reddish yellow, poor. Productive but too late.

No. 103. Six Oaks. Landreth. Ripe September 9th; fruit roundish, 6x6¼ inches, weight 4 lbs. 4 oz. Skin yellow, netted, flesh greenish white, flavor poor. Not early.

No. 105. Skillman's Netted. Henderson. Ripe September 9th; fruit oval, 5x4¾ inches, weight 1 lb. 4 oz. Skin yellowish, slightly netted, flesh greenish, poor. Productive but too late.

No. 106. Superb. Burpee. Ripe September 9th; fruit roundish, 3¾x4¼ inches, weight 1 lb. 4 oz. Skin greenish yellow, netted, flesh yellow, fair. Productive but too late.

No. 108. Salzer's Nectar of Angels. Salzer. Ripe September 2d; fruit roundish oblate, 4¾x6½ inches, weight 3 lbs. Skin light yellow, open netted, flesh pale salmon. Not of high quality but productive and early enough.

No. 114. The Captain. J. & S. Ripe September 8th;

fruit roundish, 3½x4½ inches, weight 1 lb. 14 oz. Skin yellowish, much netted, flesh greenish, excellent. Late.

No. 115. Shippers' Delight. J. & S. Ripe September 9th; fruit oblate, 1¼x3¼ inches, weight 7 oz. Skin greenish, covered with netting, flesh tinged with green, excellent. Productive but very small.

No. 119. Ward's Nectar. J. & S. Ripe September 16th; fruit round, 4x4¼ inches, weight 1 lb. 5 oz. Skin green, netted, flesh greenish, very good. Productive but too late.

No. 122. Russian Mennonite No. 2. Windom, Minnesota. Ripe September 6th; fruit oval, 6x5 inches, weight 2 lbs. Skin bright yellow, nearly smooth, flesh tinged with red, fairly good. Productive but too late.

No. 124. Russian Mennonite No. 4. Windom, Minn. Ripe August 29; fruit roundish oval, 7x5½ inches, weight 3 lbs. Skin yellow, nearly smooth, almost no netting, flesh light yellow, very fine flavor. Early.

No. 127. Extra Early Giant Prolific. Vaughan. Ripe September 16th; fruit oblate irregular, 5½x8 inches, weight 5 lbs. 10 oz. Skin yellow, much netted, flesh reddish, poor. Productive but too late.

No. 128. Superior. Vaughan. Ripe September 16th; fruit round, 5½x4¾ inches, weight 2 lbs. 2 oz. Skin yellowish green, open netting, flesh green, excellent. Too late.

No. 129. Irondequoit. Vaughan. Ripe September 16th; fruit oblate, 4½x7 inches, weight 4 lbs., 4 oz. Skin yellow, much netted, flesh greenish white, very good. Productive, but too late.

No. 131. Vaughan's Select True Jenny Lind. Vaughan. Ripe September 6th; fruit oblate, 2¾x3¾ inches, weight 11 oz. Skin yellow, covered with netting, flesh white, poor. Productive, but late.

No. 132. Thorburn's Giant. Vaughan. Ripe September 9th; fruit irregular, 5x6½ inches, weight 3 lbs., 12 oz.

Skin light yellow, smooth, flesh reddish white, poor. Productive, but too late.

No. 133. Oval Netted Gem. Vaughan. Ripe September 12th; fruit round, 3½x3½ inches, weight 14 oz. Skin green, netted, flesh greenish, excellent. Very productive and early.

No. 134. Grand Rapids. Vaughan. Ripe September 6th; fruit oval, 8½x6½ inches, weight 4 lbs. Skin dark yellow, netted, flesh reddish yellow, fair. Too late.

No. 135. New Orleans Market. Vaughan. Ripe September 16th; fruit roundish, 5¼x5¾ inches, weight 3 lbs., 9 oz. Skin yellowish, wholly covered with open netting, flesh greenish white, fair. Productive.

No. 136. Chicago Market Ordinary. Vaughan. Ripe September 16th; fruit round, 5x6 inches, weight 3 lbs., 6 oz. Skin greenish yellow, netted, flesh greenish, good. Productive, not early.

No. 140. Round Netted Gem. Vaughan. Ripe September 6th; fruit oval, 3½x3 inches, weight 12 oz. Skin yellowish green, covered with netting, flesh light green shading to dark green near rind, excellent. Productive, one of the earliest tested.

No. 142. Improved Cantaloupe. Vaughan. Ripe September 12th; fruit roundish, 4x3¾ inches, weight 1 lb., 2 oz. Skin yellow, smooth, flesh white, fair. Productive and fairly early.

No. 143. Giant Chicago Market. Vaughan. Ripe September 16th; fruit oblong, 7x6 inches, weight 5 lbs. Skin yellow, netted, flesh white, good. Productive, but too late.

U. S. Dept. Agr. No. 15. Kochanka. Russia. Ripe September 9th, fruit oval, 5½ by 5 inches, weight 3 lbs., 2 oz. Skin yellow with brownish yellow spots and open tracings of netting, very different from nutmeg tracing, flesh nearly white, juicy, very thick, and edible to the rind.

Very characteristic from the absence of open seed cavity, seeds being imbedded in the flesh. Flavor entirely distinct from other muskmelons, peculiar, though pleasant aromatic taste, rich and spicy, not pleasant to all palates. Rather late, and not very productive.

This variety is extensively used in southern Russia by confectioners for preserving in sugar. The exact method of preparing this sweetmeat will be ascertained in case the variety proves valuable further south. In a general way, the interpreter said the slices are cooked in sugar for a considerable time, and sold in a dry state.

U. S. Dept. Agr. No. 27. Mlle. Maroussia Lessevitzky. Russia. Ripe September 12th, fruit roundish oval, 6¼x5 inches, weight 3 lbs. 5 oz., surface smooth, skin yellow with green spots, flesh greenish, thick, scarcely good but sweet. Productive, but too late.

U. S. Dept. Agr. No. 28. Kochanka. Russia. Ripe September 8th; fruit round, 4x4¼ inches, weight 1 lb., 4 oz., surface yellow, partially covered with large open netting, much different from nutmeg netting, flesh reddish, very thick, seeds almost imbedded in flesh, seed cavity very small, flavor poor. Too late.

U. S. Dept. No. 30. Mme. Lydia Lessevitzky; From Russia. Ripe September 16th; fruit oblate, 3½x5 inches, weight 2 lbs. 3 oz. Surface yellow, smooth, flesh white, quality poor. Too late.

U. S. Dept. Agr. No. 42. Apricot. Moscow, Russia. Ripe September 16th; fruit round, 4½x4½ inches, weight 1 lb., 8 oz., surface smooth, slightly netted, flesh dark salmon to reddish yellow, flavor poor. Too late.

U. S. Dept. Agr. No. 52. Queen of Muskmelons. Moscow, Russia. Ripe September 16th; fruit roundish, 4½x4½ inches, weight 2 lbs. Skin greenish yellow, netted, flesh orange yellow, greenish next to the rind, very good. Too late.

U. S. Dept. Agr. No. 57. Ankelin. Moscow, Russia;

originally from Vernoe, Turkestan. Ripe September 16th; fruit oval, 4¾x4 inches. Skin yellow, almost smooth, flesh white and poor. Too late.

U. S. Dept. Agr. No. 58. Osma. Moscow, Russia. Ripe September 12th; fruit oval, 7½x5½ inches, flesh green. Too late. Used for preserves the same as No. 15.

U. S. Dept. Agr. No. 66. Lida. A Crimean variety from Moscow, Russia. Ripe September 16th; fruit oblate, 3¾x5 inches, weight 2 lbs., 2 oz. Skin smooth, yellowish, flesh orange yellow, good. Too late.

U. S. Dept. Agr. No. 102. This was an error in numbering, as it is not No. 102. Fruit roundish, 4x3½ inches, weight 1 lb. Skin hard, smooth, light yellow to white, flesh white, poor. A foreign variety. Too late.

Orange Melon. Nos. 144, 145, 146, 148 and 149 were purchased from different seedsmen under the names of Melon Peach, Climbing Orange and Vegetable Orange or Mango Melon. All proved to be identical, ripening about September 1st. The fruit is round, 3 inches in diameter, smooth, yellow, flesh white, slightly acid. (Through an oversight it was not included in Plate 4). The vines made a strong growth and were very productive. Its earliness and productiveness make it worthy of a trial in the home garden for culinary use.

This variety is also known as vine peach, orange melon, garden melon, melon apple and by other names. It is a variety of the muskmelon species.

The following is condensed from an article by Mrs. A. G. Long on "The Melon Peach and its Possibilities" in the 1899 report of the Minnesota State Horticultural Society (page 356): "The fruit is not thoroughly ripe until it detaches itself from the vine. When thoroughly ripe it may be used as a sauce in the raw state, by peeling and removing the seeds, then cutting into thin slices, adding sugar and letting it stand a half hour or more, eating it with or without cream, as desired. It makes delicious sauce, which may be improved by the addition of a little lemon extract, or better still, by a few thin slices of lemon. For sweet pickles and mangoes it is unsurpassed, and is treated in the same way as other pickles. It is excellently adapted to the making of preserves. The addition of several lemons, thinly sliced, to each pound of fruit enhances its flavor."

The receipts in the two following paragraphs are contributed by Mrs. Jas. Thornber, Brookings:

Peel, quarter, and remove seeds, cook slowly until they become clear, then add one-half pound of sugar to a quart for canning and one pound of sugar to a quart for preserving. Delicious pies are made by cooking the same as for canning, then baking.

Vegetable Pomegranate. Nos. 147 and 156 of Plate No. 4 are pomegranates. This variety of melon (Cucumis melo var. dudaim) is known as vegetable pomegranate or the Dudaim or Queen Anne's pocket melon. The fruit is round, 2 3/4 inches in diameter, mottled with yellow and brown, strongly perfumed. This curious little variety is grown for its fragrant fruit which is used for scenting rooms and wardrobes. It is not usually regarded as edible, although a jelly is sometimes made from it, as follows: Select fruit that has not become too ripe; peel, cut into quarters, cook until soft, then strain juice from pulp. To one quart of juice add an equal quantity of sugar, then boil until thick—the same as any jelly. Sugar may be added to the pulp and boiled to make pomegranate butter.

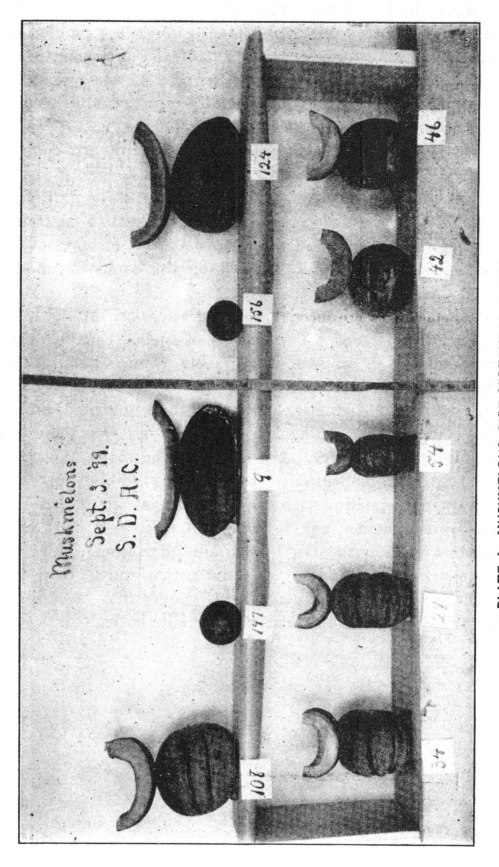

PLATE 4.—MUSKMELONS, RIPE SEPTEMBER 3, 1899.

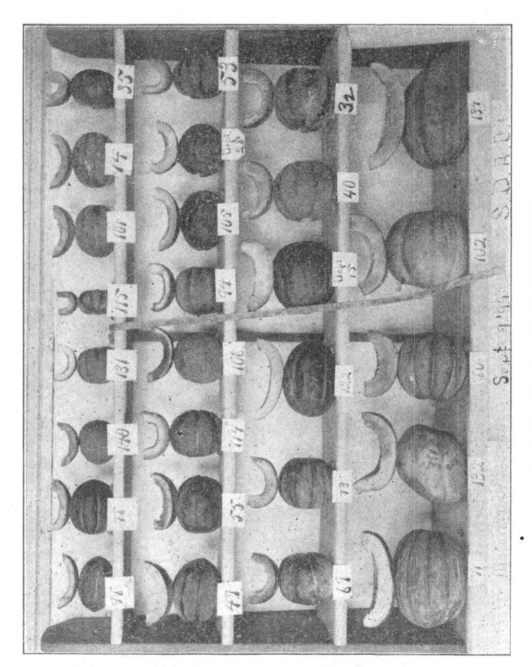

PLATE 15.—MUSKMELONS, RIPE SEPTEMBER 19, 1899.

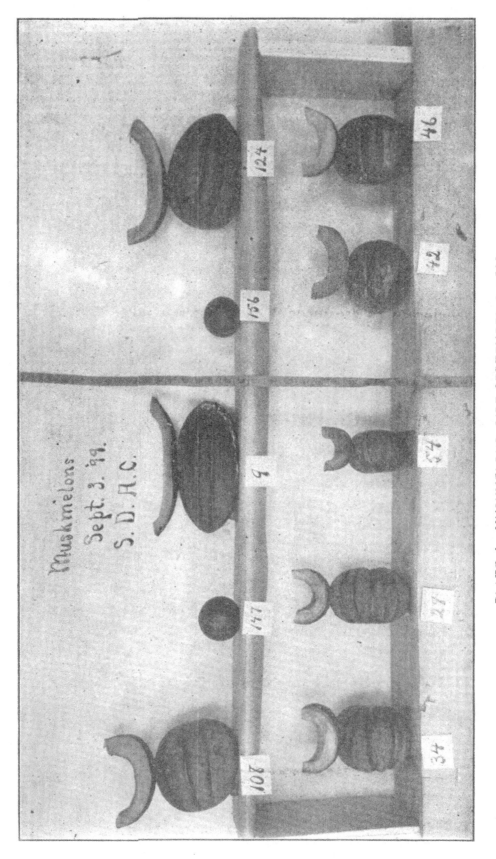

PLATE 4.—MUSKMELONS, RIPE SEPTEMBER 3, 1899.

PLATE 15.—MUSKMELONS, RIPE SEPTEMBER 19, 1899.

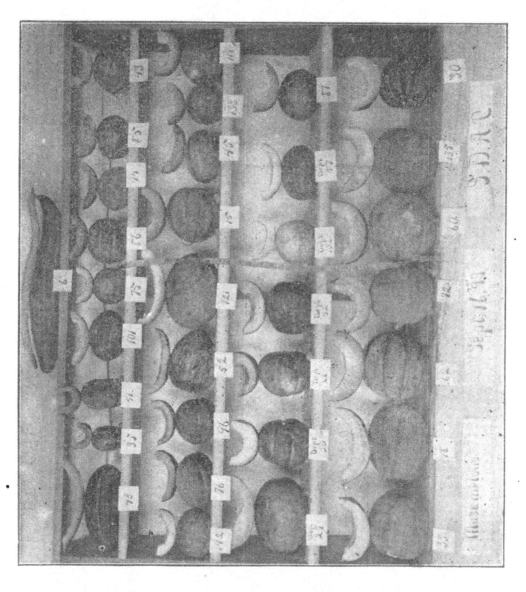

PLATE 6.—MUSKMELONS, RIPE SEPTEMBER 16, 1899.

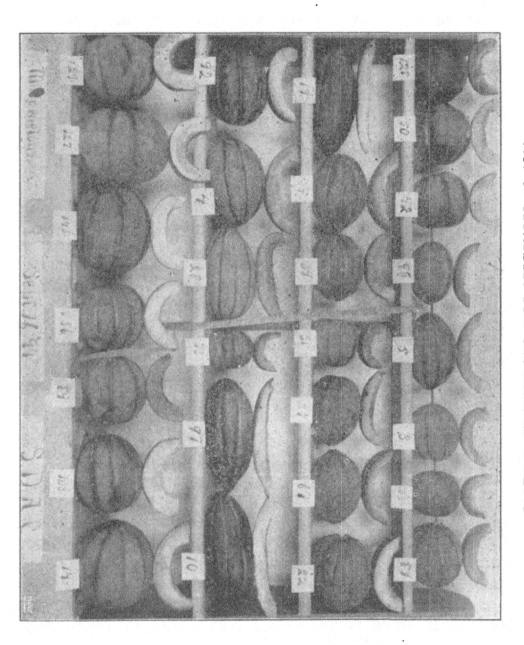

PLATE 7.—MUSKMELONS, RIPE SEPTEMBER 16, 1899.

SUMMARY OF MUSKMELONS, 1899.

PLATE 4.

Plate 4 shows eight varieties ripe by September 3:

Upper row: No. 108, No. 147, No. 9, No. 156, No. 124.

Lower row: No. 34, No. 29, No. 54, No. 42, No. 46.

Considering only quality and productiveness, No. 54, Jenny Lind, was the best.

Larger early sorts were No. 34, Earliest Ripe.

No. 29, Extra Early Citron or Nutmeg.

No. 108, Nectar of Angels.

PLATE 5.

Plate 5 shows twenty-seven varieties ripe by September 9th. With a little extra care probably all of these can be ripened in ordinary seasons.

Upper row: No. 98, No. 78, No. 140, No. 131, No. 115, No. 101, No. 14, No. 35.

Second row: No. 47, No. 55, No. 114, No. 106, No. 94, No. 105; U. S. Dept. 28, No. 53.

Third row: No. 69, No. 73. No. 122; U. S. Dept. 15, No. 40, No. 32.

Lower row: No. 71, No. 132, No. 80, No. 102, No. 134. No. 133 (see Plate 6) also belongs in this lot.

The smaller varieties proved to be earlier than the larger varieties and hence are to be preferred for localities where the growing season is short. The following varieties were both productive and of excellent quality, as well as early.

	Average Weight.
No. 32, Emerald Gem	2 lb., 2 oz.
No. 94, Prolific Nutmeg	1 lb., 4 oz.
No. 73, Newport	1 lb., 2 oz.
No. 101, Rocky Ford	1 lb.

No. 14, Burpee's Netted Gem..................14 oz.
No. 140, Round Netted Gem.....................12 oz.
No. 115, Shipper's Delight.........................7 oz.

Larger varieties, both productive and of excellent quality, but late, were:

Average Weight.

No. 40, Early Bristol......................2 lbs., 8 oz.
No. 80, N. K. & Co.'s California Cream........3 lbs., 8 oz.
No. 23, Chicago Market...........................6 lbs.

Of those with yellow flesh, No. 32, Emerald Gem, was the best of the early, and No. 80, N. K. & Co.'s California Cream, the best of the later varieties.

U. S. Dept. No. 15 is a new type of melon and deserves further trial.

PLATES 6 AND 7.

Plates Nos. 6 and 7 show 60 out of 69 varieties ripe when frost came, September 16. As all melons should be ripe by the first week in September, these cannot be regarded as early enough for safety in the northern part of this state.

PLATE 6.

Upper row: No. 6.

Second row: No. 43, No. 35, No. 51, No. 101, No. 75, No. 86, No. 14, No. 85, No. 43.

Third row: No. 142, No. 76, No. 96, No. 52, No. 121, No. 15, No. 45, No. 133, No. 119.

Fourth row: U. S. Dept. No. 27, U. S. Dept. No. 30, U. S. Dept. No. 66, U. S. Dept. No. 52, U. S. Dept. No. 102, U. Dept. No. 57, No. 87.

Lower row: No. 33, No. 18, No. 62, No. 72, No. 60, No. 135, No. 30.

PLATE 7.

Upper row: No. 128, No. 50, No. 42, No. 99, No. 5, No. 3, No. 36, No. 89.

Second row: No. 19, No. 79, No. 39, No. 31, No. 27, No. 67, No. 22.

Third row: No. 92, No. 4, No. 28, No. 73, No. 97, No. 10.

Lower row: No. 129, No. 127, No. 143, No. 136, No. 89, No. 103, No. 19.

The following also belong in this list:

No. 13, No. 61, No. 68, No. 91, No. 111, No. 121, No. 130; U. S. Dept. 42, U. S. Dept. 58.

Made in United States
North Haven, CT
13 September 2025